START WITH

Self Care

a guided journal & coloring book for relaxation
with self reflective writing prompts

Belongs to
_____

A guided journal with self care from A to Z

You can do one page a day

or

as many as you can at once.

Feel free to go in order or skip around.

You can apply the ideas on each page

to your life as often as you can

and

share them with the people you care about.

Affirmation

Write affirmations for yourself that you can start every day with:

_____

_____

_____

_____

_____

_____

_____

_____

_____

_____

_____

_____

_____

_____

_____

_____

_____

Complete the following sentences:

I am a _____ person
I forgive myself for_____
I _____ my own attitude.

Write about a time that you didn't believe in yourself:

_____

_____

_____

_____

_____

_____

_____

What will you do differently if you feel that way again?

_____

_____

_____

_____

_____

_____

_____

_____

_____

Believe

Confidence

Define what confidence means to you:

List as many ideas as you can about what will make you a more confident person:

_____
_____
_____
_____
_____
_____
_____
_____
_____
_____
_____
_____
_____

Discovering new things like groups with similar interests as you, can be a great way to kick start your personal growth.
Write about new things you would like to learn about:

_____

_____

_____

_____

_____

_____

_____

_____

_____

_____

_____

_____

_____

How can you find others who want to learn similar things as you?

Discover

Empower

Empowerment means you are becoming stronger and more powerful.
List all the things that are true about you!

I am	I am not

What were you up to a year ago?
(You can write, draw or cut and glue pictures in the box)

Where do you want to be a year from now?
(You can write, draw or cut and glue pictures in the box)

Flourish

Goals

What are your goals for the future and how do you plan to achieve them?

(You can set big or small goals)

GOAL	STRATEGY

What you put inside your body matters. Plan out healthy meals for a week

(Challenge yourself to plan your meals every week from now on)

	Breakfast	Lunch	Dinner
Monday			
Tuesday			
Wednesday			
Thursday			
Friday			
Saturday			
Sunday			

Healthy

I

Increase

What do you need more of in order to be your best self?

_____

_____

_____

_____

_____

_____

_____

Who are the people around you
that can support you in getting what you need?

_____

_____

_____

_____

_____

_____

_____

_____

_____

_____

_____

_____

_____

For each phrase, write how this inspires your self-love journey

"Practice makes progress"

_____
_____
_____
_____
_____

"Do not be afraid to start again"

_____
_____
_____
_____
_____

"Good things take time"

_____
_____
_____
_____
_____

Journey

K

Kind

Be kind to yourself
&
Be kind to others

How can you apply this idea everyday?

_____

_____

_____

_____

_____

_____

_____

_____

_____

_____

_____

_____

_____

_____

_____

_____

_____

_____

_____

_____

Listen to positive words as much as possible.
Write a playlist of music that gets you inspired and uplifted!

Title	Artist

Listen

Meditate

Meditate for 10 minutes:

- Become aware of the present moment and your environment
- Release any worries or tension in your body
- Accept whatever is happening
- Focus on your body at the moment; your breathe, your senses and your thoughts

How do you feel?

Spend time outdoors today and write down the
wonderful things that you hardly notice on other days:

_____

_____

_____

_____

_____

_____

_____

_____

_____

_____

_____

_____

_____

_____

_____

_____

_____

_____

_____

_____

_____

_____

_____

Nature

Organize

Choose an area in your life or space that needs to be organized and clear out any mess.

How will you be able to keep it up?

_____

_____

_____

_____

_____

_____

_____

_____

_____

_____

_____

_____

_____

_____

_____

_____

_____

_____

_____

_____

_____

_____

_____

List 5 ways you can pamper yourself

Now treat yourself to it!

Pamper

Quiet

Take quiet time for yourself everyday.
Plan out your daily schedule to ensure your quiet time is blocked off

	M	T	W	T	F	S	S
6a							
7a							
8a							
9a							
10a							
11a							
12p							
1p							
2p							
3p							
4p							
5p							
6p							
7p							
8p							
9p							
10p							

What types of books do you enjoy reading and why?

_____

_____

_____

_____

_____

_____

_____

_____

_____

_____

_____

_____

Complete the following sentences:

My favorite book is _____.

It is written by _____.

The next book I want to read is titled _____ by _____.

Read

Smile

Write or draw
the things that bring you joy:

Try something new today.
How will it make you feel about yourself?

_____

_____

_____

_____

_____

_____

_____

_____

_____

_____

_____

_____

_____

_____

_____

_____

_____

_____

_____

_____

Try

Unplug

List 10 things you can do when taking a break from online / social media:

1)
_____
2)
_____
3)
_____
4)
_____
5)
_____
6)
_____
7)
_____
8)
_____
9)
_____
10)
_____

Vision Board

Write

Write a letter to your future self:

_____

_____

_____

_____

_____

_____

_____

_____

_____

_____

_____

_____

_____

_____

_____

_____

_____

_____

_____

_____

_____

Look up the definition of "xenial" and explain it in your own words:

_____

_____

_____

_____

_____

_____

How can you relate this to your life?

_____

_____

_____

_____

_____

_____

_____

_____

_____

_____

_____

_____

_____

_____

Xenial

Yoga

Write you favorite yoga quotes:

Decorate the yoga mat:

Gratitude
I am thankful for:

Learn what "zingy" means and write how
you can make it part of who you are?

_____

_____

_____

_____

_____

_____

_____

_____

_____

_____

_____

_____

_____

_____

_____

_____

_____

_____

_____

_____

_____

_____

_____

Zingy

Be proud of who you are becoming!

If you enjoyed this journal be sure to share with others!